100 Handy Budget Tips

Carmel McCartin

100 Handy Budget Tips

Published 2013 by Budget Bitch Australia

Copyright © 2013 Carmel McCartin

Editing & Formatting: Michael Betts

Publisher: Budget Bitch Pty Ltd

ABN 65 123 977 480

Kingston Road Thurgoona NSW 2640

Australia`

www.BudgetBitch.com.au

ISBN 978 0 9875113 3 1

Disclaimer: The material contained in this book is the personal opinions of the author and is for general reference. The information and content in this book is provided on an 'as is' basis and the author makes no warranty with respect to information available within this book; assumes no legal liability or responsibility whatsoever for the accuracy, completeness, or usefulness of any such information; and does not represent that its use would not infringe privately owned rights or legislation. The author disclaims all warranties, express and implied, including the warranties of merchantability and fitness for a particular purpose. The Publisher does not warrant that the information is free from errors or omissions. To the maximum extent permitted by law, Budget Bitch Pty Ltd does not accept any liability for any loss, damage, costs or expenses incurred by you in connection with the contents of this book.

Accuracy and completeness of information: While reasonable efforts are taken to ensure the accuracy and integrity of all information provided here, the author is not responsible for misprints, out-of-date information or errors. The content included in this book has been compiled from a variety of sources and is subject to change without notice as are any offerings, products, programs, services or technical information described in this book. The author makes no warranty, express or implied, or assumes any legal liability or responsibility for the accuracy, completeness or quality of any information contained within this book.

No Endorsement: The inclusion in this book of any reference to any website, entity, product or service by trade name, trademark, manufacturer or otherwise does not necessarily constitute or imply an endorsement or recommendation by the author. Any access, use or engagement of, or other dealings with such website, entity, product or service shall be solely at the users own risk. No company or product included in this book is affiliated with the author, and the author expressly states that there is no express or implied endorsement of the book by any company mentioned herein.

This book is based on the author's research and experiences. Please use your own judgement as to whether it is safe and appropriate for you and your situation before following any instruction in this book.

Contents

Foreword

Having a budget doesn't mean being a cheapskate. Nor does it mean you must live frugally. It's about making the most of the money you have today.

This book holds a simple collection of 100 Handy Budget Tips. Some of them are old, some are new. Some of these tips have been passed down through my family, whilst others have been collected and collated from all over the world.

There are some tips that I've written for you and some that I've learned the hard way. All of them are useful.

There's no doubt that you will have heard or learned some of these Budget Tips before. Just reading them again will remind you of their worth.

This is a great quick-reference guide to help you make it easier to manage your money.

"A budget is like a GPS - it always lets you know your position." ~ B.B.

Lifestyle

Entertainment
Holidays & Travel
Camping
Health & Fitness
Fashion
Beauty
Being Romantic
Transport & Cars
Fuel

Entertainment

1. Picnics can be a great form of inexpensive entertainment - you only need a nice day, some sandwiches, drinks and maybe a ball to throw around.

2. Plan a meal, invite your friends over and ask them to not only bring some of the ingredients, but tell them that they can help with the cooking. It's a very social activity.

3. Always, take your own food & drinks when visiting theme parks, the zoo, or anywhere there is an admission fee. This will help to keep the cost of an outing to a minimum.

Holidays and Travel

4. Book your airline flights well in advance because as your holiday draws closer, cheaper departure dates and times may no longer be available.

5. If you plan to stay in a city a long time, renting an apartment can be a good option. Furnished apartments are usually cheaper than hotels and, you'll get the comforts of home without spending a lot of money.

6. Weigh your suitcase on the bathroom scales before you leave home to make sure you don't get hit for excess baggage charges when checking in for your flight.

Camping

7. Food and drinks can be kept cool in a cooler/esky/ portable fridge. Keep the ice in their bags, and open the lid as few times as possible. This will keep the cool air in, which will keep the ice frozen longer.

8. After showering, wipe yourself with a 'chux' cloth (or similar) to remove excess water. Then dry off with your towel. Doing this will mean that your towels are fresher for longer, before you need to launder them.

Health and Fitness

9. Reducing the size of your food portions will save calories and also save money on the grocery bill.

10. Rent large personal gym equipment items instead of buying them. It's cheaper to 'hire and use' than it is to 'purchase and store away'.

11. Snack smarter by taking your own snack home rather than hitting the vending machines. It's much more expensive to buy individual snacks from the machines than to portion out servings from full-size packages into zipper bags.

Fashion

12.   You must try on every article of clothing
        that you want to buy. Impulse buying is a
        bad habit that often results in a regretful
        purchase of ill-fitting, ugly clothes you
        simply don't want once you get home.

13.   Unless you're constantly undressing in
        public - underwear does not need to be
        brand named. Many of the cheaper brands
        are better value.

14.   Check the care labels on each garment. If
        your money is tight, you may find it
        difficult to afford a weekly dry-cleaning
        bill.

Beauty

15. You don't need to pay for fancy packaging and a popular brand name - most shampoos, shower gels and facial cleansers have got identical ingredients in them (read the labels on the back).

16. Learn to give yourself a manicure. For the price of one manicure, you can buy a kit that will last you several months.

Being Romantic

17. Leave little love notes everywhere. Putting one in the middle of the lunchtime sandwich will definitely get a reaction.

18. Have dinner on the roof, with some candles. Warning! This doesn't work if your roof slopes sharply

Transport and Cars

19. If you have a small chip on your car windscreen, try to get it fixed as soon as possible. Fixing an entire windscreen will cost much more than fixing a minor chip.

20. Downsize your car and save money; not only in monthly payments but also in maintenance, insurance and operating expenses.

21. If you have to drive to work and you live near other work colleagues, arrange to car-pool and share the petrol and parking costs with your friends.

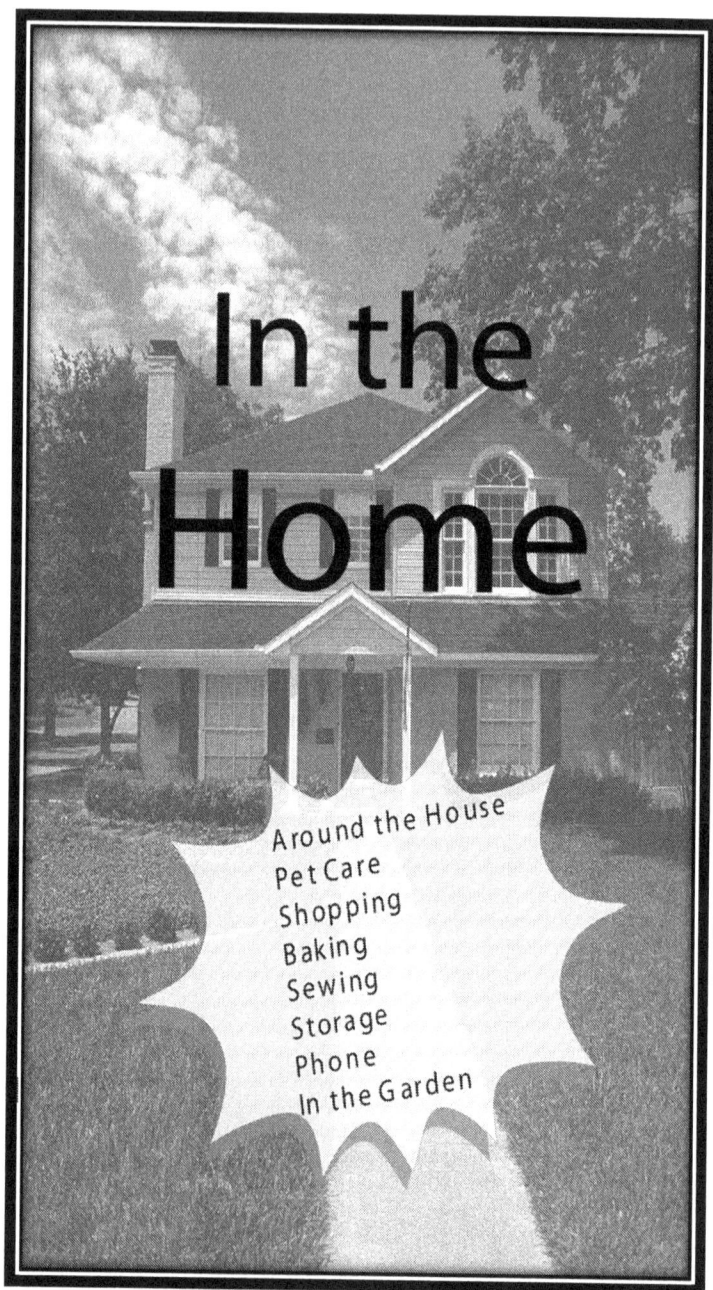

In the Home

Around the House
Pet Care
Shopping
Baking
Sewing
Storage
Phone
In the Garden

Around the House

24.   Make a list of all annual maintenance items for your home such as the air-conditioner, heater, hot water service, etc. Include appliances such as the lawn mower, barbecue, and so on. Being prepared and working in a proactive manner can save you unnecessary expenses.

25.   Trade services – the old bartering system is a great way to save money. E.g. give a neighbour a haircut (if that's your regular job) in return for a car service (if that's their regular job).

26.   Generic medicines can save you hundreds of dollars per year. If you're not sure about the ingredients, ask your chemist.

Pet Care

27. Over feeding not only fattens your dog (which leads to expensive veterinary bills) but is also a waste of expensive dog food.

28. Buy a good quality grooming kit and clip your pet's coat regularly. Small dogs cost an average of $50 each time if you don't do this yourself. You'll recoup the money for the clippers very quickly.

29. Holiday accommodation for pets is not cheap. Find another pet owner who is willing to care for your pet whilst you're away; in return for you reciprocating the favour.

Shopping

30. Decide what you are looking to buy. Don't just wander the shops waiting for inspiration. Decide before you go what it is that you will purchase.

31. Don't be frightened of 'second-hand shops'. If it's good enough to donate your preloved goods, then surely it's good enough to shop there also.

32. Convert your weekly supermarket allocation into store gift cards. You won't be able to overspend.

Baking

33. Find recipes that let you use what's in the cupboard. That end-of-the-bag coconut, dried fruit or white chocolate chips purchased at an earlier time, or a box of high fibre cereal pushed to the back of the cupboard can find their way into cookies, bars, quick breads and muffins.

34. It may be cheaper buying food in bulk, but unless you have a plan to use it all, you're wasting your money and food.

Sewing

35.   You can find cheap fabric at Thrift stores.
      Manufacturers often donate rolls of fabric
      at the end of the season - you just have to
      find the stores that are the recipients of this
      gift.

36.   Work out how much you can afford to
      spend before buying a sewing machine.
      There are always excellent second-hand
      machines available. Remember it's the skill
      level that makes the garment - not the
      machine.

Storage

37. Ice cube trays make excellent multi-purpose storage devices; allowing you to hold the tiniest trinkets, office supplies, and craft components in their place.

38. Second-hand wardrobes make great storage places in the garden shed or the workshop.

Phone

39. Don't choose any phone plan (mobile or fixed line) that locks you into a contract for 1 or 2 years. New & better phone deals are coming onto the market every day and if you have the ability to leave at any time then this forces the phone company to ensure that your bills are competitively priced and you're not over-charged.

40. If you only use your mobile phone for occasional calls, a prepaid plan may be the cheapest service option for you. Shop around and you could spend as little as $20 every three months.

In the Garden

41.   Swap cuttings from your garden with other gardeners. This is the most inexpensive way to get new plants. Most gardeners are more than willing to share.

42.   Keep your eye out for secondhand garden tools and furniture. You'll be surprised how many are available online and at garage sales.

43.   Compost your garden leftovers as well as your fruit and vegetable scraps from the kitchen. Don't forget that used coffee grounds are great for composting, as are grass clippings and dead leaves. Compost is great for your gardening budget.

Families

Babies
Kids Birthday Parties
Back to School

Babies

44. Young babies have very simple needs. They need warmth, shelter, milk, cuddles and love so that they can thrive. The rest is just window dressing. Remembering this will help your budget.

45. Don't overspend on baby toiletries - baby cream, baby powder, baby shampoo. Babies already have beautiful skin, and nobody will ever know if you use the generic brand of these products.

46. Wipe warmers, fancy rompers, colourful plastic nappy disposal bags, and baby seats and positioners are all great extras to have but they're not really necessary. Stick with the basics and you'll have more money for the important stuff.

Kids Birthday Parties

47.   Host the party at your home. If your house is too small, make use of a public playground or park.

48.   If you really must have party favours to take home – make some plain cupcakes that the children can decorate at the party.

49.   Party games don't have to cost money – musical chairs, pass the parcel with a few homemade biscuits inside, and treasure hunts using the birthday cake as the hidden treasure.

Back to School

50.   Identify your child's belongings - every pencil, crayon and marker. If you don't, they may end up in the collection box at school, and so will your money.

51.   Buy basics such as t-shirts, socks, underwear, shorts and trousers in multiples when they are on sale. Buying out of season saves you the most money, but make sure to calculate the right size for the proper season when buying ahead for fast growing children.

52.   You can save some serious dollars on your budget if you buy in bulk. Get together with some of the other parents and set a date to go shopping at a large wholesale discounter. You'll be able to get what you need, below retail prices.

Celebrations

Planning
Gifts
Food
Drinks
Decorations
Easter

Planning

53.   Early preparation for your celebrations will help save the last-minute rush; which always costs you more in the long run.

54.   Don't forget that the best party memories are about people and events - the size and cost of the gifts are insignificant.

Gifts

55. Give vouchers – lawn mowing; painting;
     baby-sitting; house cleaning etc. Nowadays
     people are time poor, not possession poor

56. Choose a theme for your gifts – calendars,
     books, chocolates, homemade treats, socks,
     pens, glasses, pillows, etc.

57. Don't forget that the best party memories
     are about people and events - the size and
     cost of the gifts are insignificant.

Food

58. Share the cooking – ask guests to participate by contributing a part of the menu. Don't forget that there are other people who would love to share their 'family favourite'.

59. Store brands are great for side dishes and salads etc. - nobody will even realise!

Drinks

60. Check out the 'end-of-bin' sales in your local liquor shop. There are heaps of great wines to be found at fabulous prices.

61. A lot of money is spent on alcohol for celebrations. Try serving guests a festive glass of punch – you can even stretch out servings with apple juice.

Decorations

62. Wrap gifts in bright and glossy junk mail -
     it all ends up in the same place in the end!

63. Give an extra gift by wrapping small gifts
     in hankies or cloth napkins.

Easter

64.   Kits with candy moulds can be obtained at your local craft or department store. Not only will the cost of the chocolate be cheaper per kilo to make them, you will be able to use the kits for many years to come.

65.   Consider buying multi-purpose containers instead of the traditional Easter baskets - such as sand buckets, flower pots, storage containers, etc. This way you will be giving the Easter basket recipient an extra gift.

Weddings

Outfits
Beauty Hints
The Ceremony
Flowers
The Reception
Cake
Photography
The Honeymoon

Outfits

66. It's critical that you remember that you will probably only wear these clothes once. Ask your attendants to contribute financially to the clothes they will wear (after all they do get to keep them) or perhaps pick a themed wedding - fancy costumes are much cheaper than wedding attire.

67. Bridal gown cleaning is expensive. When purchasing a pre-loved item, don't pick the one that has a dirty hem or needs cleaning.

68. Many of the big bridal shops have huge sales once a year, make sure you attend.

Beauty Hints

69. Consider approaching a hairdressing and/or beauty college and offering your wedding as a project. The costs will be minimal and all work is supervised.

70. If hair accessories are going to be put in anyone's hair, make sure you buy them yourself. If you leave this up to the hair stylist it'll cost more.

The Ceremony

71.   Consider getting married on any day other than a Saturday. You'll be surprised at how much this will cut the costs of everything.

72.   Focus on what you want rather than what everybody seems to tell you that you should have. All those extras cost dollars.

73.   It is important that your wedding invitations are special; however there is no need to go overboard as your guests will remember your ceremony and wedding reception more than the invitation.

Flowers

74. You don't have to spend a lot of money in order to have beautiful flowers for your wedding. All you need to do is plan carefully, order well in advance and not be too fussy by wanting flowers that are out of season.

75. Silk flowers save you a lot of money and they're already preserved. The bride can have fresh flowers, but there really isn't any need for everyone else to have them.

The Reception

76.   If you have a small budget consider a brunch reception as the food cost is usually a lot less and your guests will usually not drink as much.

77.   You don't need to have a 'rehearsal dinner'. Seriously, you'll all be getting together for eats and drinks on the day of the wedding anyway. Cut the expense!

78.   If you're having a wedding with 75 guests or under, consider having your reception at your favourite restaurant. You will already know the staff and how good the food is.

The Cake

79. Ask a cake decorating class if they'd like to take on your wedding cake as a project. You pay for the materials of course.

80. It can be an enormous help to your budget if you combine your wedding cake as part of your meal and perhaps use it as dessert.

Photography

81. Approach a photography school and ask if their students might like to use your wedding as a project. Offer to purchase their best shots.

82. The full length framed photo is gorgeous for the first few years, but you'll need a very large wall to hang it on and it'll probably cost you the same as a mortgage payment. Hang onto your money for other things.

The Honeymoon

83. Don't book the 'honeymoon suite'. Generally the only difference between that and any other nice room is the gift of a bottle of bubbly and chocolates.

84. Your wedding budget should also include your honeymoon. Work out which priorities are most important and allocate the money accordingly. You may be able to spend less on some aspects of your wedding so that more of your budget can go towards your honeymoon.

Helping the Environment

Cooling
Heating
Electricity
Refrigeration
Saving the Planet

Cooling

85. Avoid landscaping with lots of unshaded rock, cement, or asphalt on the southern or western sides. It increases the temperature around the house and radiates heat to the house after the sun has set.

86. If it's possible, place your air-conditioning unit in a cool or shaded area. If the unit is in direct sunlight, it uses more energy to cool your house.

Heating

87. Only heat the space that you are in. Central heating is great, but if your family only uses one or two rooms then you are throwing away vast amounts of energy and money to heat the entire house.

88. Draw your curtains as soon as it gets dark – windows lose more heat than walls and covering them with your curtains will ensure that you keep as much of your heat inside as possible. If you don't have curtains, think about getting some.

89. Thermal underwear is excellent! It might look a bit daggy, but nobody sees it and it's better to be warm and look happy than feel cold and look miserable.

Electricity

90. Purchase energy efficient white goods (washing machines, tumble dryers, fridges etc.). Although they may cost a little more initially, the cost savings in electricity will cover that many times over.

91. Cook many items at the same time when your electric oven is already hot. You have more than rack in your oven, use 2 or more at the same time.

92. Heat only as much water in an electric kettle as you require for drinks and cooking.

Refrigeration

93. Vacuum clean the condenser coils at the back or underneath your fridge or freezer. Accumulated fluff/dust reduces their efficiency by up to 25%, adding that cost to your electricity bill.

94. Open the door only when necessary. Don't let your teenager prop on the door whilst deciding what to eat/drink.

Saving the Planet

95.   Where possible whilst wrapping, storing or cleaning - use cloth instead of paper.

96.   Use rags for cleaning and polishing, instead of paper towels.

97.   Use real dinnerware instead of paper plates and cups.

Money

Personal Finances
Small Business

Personal finances

98.   Use cash! Paying by cash will make you think twice about breaking a $50 note. It will also make you more aware about where your money is going.

99.   Get an empty jar for loose coins. Every time you get home put any coins you may have in your pocket or purse into the jar. It won't make you a millionaire but it all adds up over time.

100.   Teaching your kids how to budget and save money is more valuable than you just building up a bank account for them. Make it a family project and that way everyone will feel comfortable discussing money matters.

About the Author

Carmel McCartin is an accomplished writer and speaker. Her articles have been published both online and in the print media. This is her third book.

She established the Budget Bitch Company in 2007 after two years research whilst working as a personal budget consultant. Carmel has appeared on television as a specialist budgeting reporter and is a regular commentator on local and current budgeting issues.

As Australia's #1 Budget Guru she has been called "The Chick who takes no crap from anyone" and "the next person to dabble with your wallet".

The tips in this book provide a great start for anyone serious about getting their personal finances in order.

If you enjoyed 100 Handy Budget Tips and want more, then you can purchase 1001 Budget Tips – available now!

http://www.1001budgettips.com.au

Your Amazing Itty Bitty® "After" Financial Checklist

15 Important Actions to Complete After the Loss of a Loved One

Losing a loved one is shocking and devastating. Losing a loved one without having pertinent records in place makes a difficult situation even worse. This Itty Bitty® Book is intended to get you thinking and talking to the right people and taking actions that will smooth the transition for you.

This book is for you, whether you:

- are thinking ahead regarding your own estate,
- have lost a spouse, parent, friend or other family member,
- are aware of a terminal condition and trying to prepare for what is to come, or
- are unsure about what is involved after the loss of a loved one and want to become more aware.

If you may eventually be involved in taking care of financial matters after the loss of a loved one, pick up this vitally important and informative book today.

Your Amazing
Itty Bitty®
"After" Financial
Checklist

15 Important Actions to Complete
After the Loss of a Loved One

Marie Burns, CFP®

Published by Itty Bitty® Publishing
A subsidiary of S&P Productions, Inc.

Printed in the United States of America

Itty Bitty® Publishing
311 Main Street, Suite D
El Segundo, CA 90245
(310) 640-8885

ISBN: 978-0-9996519-3-3

This booklet is intended to be informational only
and is not intended to be construed as tax,
financial or legal advice. Readers should consult
their own tax, financial and legal advisors who
are licensed in their state of residence and
familiar with their personal situation.

Dedication

This book is dedicated to families and individuals to reduce their financial stress and help them move forward during an already difficult time.

Drop by our Itty Bitty® Publishing website to learn more.

www.ittybittypublishing.com

or visit Marie Burns at

www.**MindMoneyMotion**.com

Table of Contents

Introduction

This Itty Bitty® Book is designed to help you take action on some financial steps that are best completed

- within the first few days,
- after the first couple weeks,
- and over the next few months

after the loss of a loved one.

It is not uncommon, and it is very normal, to look back to the time shortly after someone's death and not remember saying or doing something that you know you did or were told that you did. When the brain is in trauma mode, it may "shut the door" to the logical side of the brain and camp out in the emotional side, unable to remember clearly for a period of time.

Having a process, documented notes, and an ordered action list can help you move forward with getting things updated while the brain is still recovering. Relying on the help of trusted family, friends and advisors is a must as well.

This Itty Bitty® Book will remind you not to make any major decisions, financially or otherwise, for 6-12 months after the loss of a loved one. In the meantime, you can take care of getting your financial house back in order by following the 15 steps in this book.

Step 1
The First Few Days:
Notify Family And Friends

Start a dated notebook now to log your activities. It's likely you will not remember many details for a period of time. Your first entry is who to notify about the death.

1. Doctor. A physician needs to be involved in declaring the date and time of death. If 911 has to be called, have in hand a do-not-resuscitate document if it exists. Without one, paramedics generally must start emergency procedures and, except where permitted to pronounce death, take the person to an emergency room for a doctor to make the declaration.
2. Family members. You may ask some family to help notify others.
3. Friends and neighbors. If the loved one was ill, he or she may have made a list of who should be contacted.
4. Clergy. You may need to set an appointment to discuss final celebration details as well.
5. Employer. Request any necessary paperwork when making this call.

Notifying Family And Friends Of A Death

Learning about the death of a loved one can be one of the most traumatic events in a person's life. Being the bearer of the news can be an incredibly emotional task and can wear many people out after only a few calls or visits, so consider options for spreading the word that a loved one has died recently:

- Phone Tree---Ask family members or close friends if they would mind making some calls
- Email---This can still be somewhat personal, yet you can reach a larger number of people at the same time. Make sure you've personally notified close family before you send a group email so no one is offended.
- Social Media---Lastly, after you've notified everyone that needs a personal contact, Facebook can be another way to notify friends so that they can get information about the memorial service. Facebook also has a Memorialization form online that can be used to delete a deceased person's account.

Step 2
The First Few Days:
Understand And Plan For Final Wishes

Hopefully, there is a Final Disposition form or something similar in writing that indicates your loved one's final wishes regarding cremation vs. burial, memorial preferences, etc.

1. Locate and review any estate planning documents that address final wishes (Health Care Directives, Final Disposition, etc.)
2. www.funerals.org can be a helpful resource regarding planning final services.
3. Order 10-20 certified copies of the death certificate (often available from the funeral home or county office). When dealing with paperwork later, you will need these certificates for most accounts and policies you have to deal with.
4. Place an obituary in relevant papers.
5. Make arrangements for someone to stay at the house during the service since obituary and funeral notices can alert burglars to empty homes.
6. Plan for all the details around the memorial service.

3

Things to Think About When Planning A Memorial Service

- Decide on an overall theme or main message that can be reflected in the music, decorations, location, etc.
- Pick a location that will accommodate and be convenient for the number of people attending.
- Think about a date that considers travel time for guests.
- Choose a person or people to lead the services.
- Determine whether flowers vs. donations or live plants vs. flowers will be preferred.
- Select and request readers/speakers and musicians.
- Gather photographs or other memorabilia to display.
- Address how memorial gifts should be provided.
- Ask for and accept offers to help with all of the above.

Step 3
The First Few Days: Call
The Appropriate Offices

Call the Social Security Office at 800-772-1213 to report a death (and the Veteran's Affairs Office or U.S. Office of Personnel Management (federal employee) if applicable).

1. Stop the deceased's deposits. The last deposit may need to be withdrawn if received after the date of death.
2. Claim the $255 death benefit if you are the surviving spouse.
3. Consider the option of applying for survivor benefits if you are an eligible surviving spouse and/or have minor children.
4. The Social Security Office will automatically notify Medicare, if applicable.

Social Security After A Death

- You cannot report a death or apply for survivor benefits online.
- There may be limits on how much you can earn while receiving benefits.
- Remarriage can affect survivor benefits.
- Pension income can impact survivor benefits.
- Your own retirement benefits should be considered when determining the best option for claiming survivor benefits.
- The Social Security Program rules may change over time, so it is best to make an appointment to meet with a representative at the Social Security Office to understand options and benefits.
- Discuss your options with your tax and financial advisors to maximize your income for the most tax efficiency **before** filing an election with the Social Security Office.

When applying for Social Security benefits, have available your spouse's birth and death certificates and your marriage certificate (if applicable), birth certificates of any dependent children, Social Security numbers, and copies of your spouse's most recent federal income tax return.

Step 4
The First Few Days:
Deal With The Emotional Brain

Emotions can seem to make a brain confused or think irrationally. Regardless of how the brain actually works, be aware that it is normal to have difficulty remembering things during this time, so write everything down.

1. Start and keep an ongoing notebook to document dates/times of all calls and the content of important conversations and meetings.
2. You may find it helpful to leave a separate notebook at the entrance of your home to log all visitors, deliveries, etc.
3. A helping hand can make a huge difference in easing the burden so delegate and accept assistance from those you trust.

Acknowledgment Cards After A Loss

Grief is devastating and exhausting in itself. After final services are over, the thought of handwriting an often large volume of notes for memorial cards or gifts, can feel overwhelming.

- Do you plan to send out cards? If so, who and how will you record and keep track of the gifts, names and addresses?
- Is there someone who can assist you with tracking and sending out the cards?
- Sometimes banks receive memorial gifts directly, but may not keep helpful records of the name and address of the donors – can that be prevented?
- If you decide not to send out cards, can you express gratitude instead with an acknowledgement placed near the cards/gifts, a note in the program, personal conversations, etc.?

There is no right or wrong decision on this. In a small community, an ad in the local paper may be appropriate. A short video memorial posted on Facebook with heartfelt words might be a solution. The main point is to think about it in advance so you can act on that decision without undue added stress at the appropriate time. Most especially, those who have experienced grief before will understand whatever you decide.

Step 5
The First Few Days:
Contact Your Estate Planning Attorney

You are not ready to have lengthy conversations right now, but call the estate planning attorney's office to set an appointment for 2-3 weeks out. Sometimes, this is the same attorney who drafted the will and/or trust documents.

1. Let the attorney's office know you are calling to make them aware of someone's passing and set an appointment to discuss further.
2. Ask to clarify which account should be used to pay for funeral and other short-term expenses.
3. They may share other specific information you should be aware of promptly.
4. Ask specifically what they would like you to bring to your upcoming meeting.

A Few General Things To Keep In Mind After Death

- No one should take or begin distributing anything until after the attorney meeting where roles and next steps can be clarified. It's wise to keep cash and valuables in locked locations.
- Keep lines of communication open so those involved understand the process and time involved; this can help avoid misinformation and suspicion.
- Set realistic expectations (for yourself and others); depending on the complexity of the assets involved, the process of finalizing the estate can take from three months to three years.
- Realize that almost everything that needs to be taken care of requires some paperwork to be signed, even when documents were prepared and updated correctly in advance, it is still a process that will take some time.

As an executor, there is fiduciary liability and exposure to you, personally, if you do not follow the terms of the will exactly. Seeking professional support from an estate planning attorney is a good idea.

Step 6
The First Couple Weeks:
Set Appointments With Your Advisors

It is important to get the estate overview meeting with the attorney completed first (a month or so after the death). Then you can take what you learned from that meeting with you to meet with the tax and financial advisor. Set those appointments now so they are on the calendar.

1. Start a file for all receipts and start an expense log to track bills paid after death. Take that with you to meet with the tax advisor, after meeting with the attorney.
2. Go to the bank to request date of death values on all accounts. You may need to go back again later after the attorney meeting to update account titles and beneficiaries at the bank as well.
3. If you are a surviving spouse, it is often a good idea to keep a joint checking account open until the estate settlement process is complete.
4. Call your financial advisor to request date of death values of all accounts in writing and to set up an appointment (for after you meet with the attorney).

Tips For Setting Appointments

- Use your log to write down the details: time, date, address of meeting, name of person you are meeting with, any directions as needed.
- Ask in advance what you should bring to the meeting and add those notes to your log.
- If there are specific concerns you have, let them know when you set the appointment about the agenda items that you want to be sure to have addressed.
- You may want to request a reminder call, email or text with the details of the appointment.
- Write your appointment down on a visible calendar as well as entering it into your phone and in your log.
- Plan to leave for your advisor meetings well in advance so you avoid feeling rushed and frazzled upon arrival; the agenda and circumstances are stressful enough.

Step 7
The First Couple Weeks:
Notify All Insurance Companies

Notify all insurance agents/companies to determine if coverage needs to be adjusted, terminated, or if benefits are to be paid out.

1. Hopefully there is already a list of all insurance providers, the policy numbers and contact information for you to call. Otherwise you will need to compile it.
2. Call each agent/company to notify them of the death and determine what is required to adjust, terminate or receive benefits from the policy.
3. When asked to provide a death certificate, clarify if it can be a copy or if it needs to be a certified death certificate. If certified, request that it be mailed back to you after processing to avoid having to order more later.
4. Keep notes in your log of the date, time and phone number you called, name of who you spoke to, information provided and next steps---in case you need to call again later.

Common Types Of Insurance That Should Be Notified

- Life
- Accident, if applicable
- Health/dental/vision
- Auto
- Home
- Long-term care
- Umbrella liability
- Disability (short- and long-term)

Don't forget the small policies, like the $1,000 death benefit typically offered on some bank accounts or credit cards.

Step 8
The First Month:
Inform Billers and Creditors

Notify billers (utilities, internet provider, cable company, etc.) and creditors (loan, mortgage and credit card providers) of death.

1. Make notes in your log of the details of each call.
2. Some payments may need to stop or be adjusted due to death.
3. Automatic payment details may need to be updated.
4. Accounts may need to be re-titled with new ownership or closed.
5. Inquire about whether any of the loans or credit card balances are automatically zeroed out in the event of death.
6. Notify all three credit reporting agencies and request a report on the deceased person. Make a note to contact them again several months down the road to request another copy of the reports in a new calendar year, to see if there has been any fraudulent activity after death.

Requesting A Free Annual Credit Report

You can request an annual free credit report from all three credit reporting agencies (Equifax, Experian and TransUnion) via any one of these three methods:

- Online at www.annualcreditreport.com
- By calling: (877) 322-8228
- By mail to: Annual Credit Report Request Service, P.O. Box 105281, Atlanta, GA 30348-5281

Step 9
The First Month:
Update Your Net Worth Statement

Before you see the attorney, tax advisor or financial advisor, you want to take the time to update your Net Worth Statement (current list of what you own and what you owe) so you can take it with you to those meetings.

1. Check out Net Worth Statement formats online, or use a yellow pad to list what you own on the left and what you owe on the right side.
2. Date the Net Worth Statement and list all personal property and account names (referred to as assets) and their current market values, as well as balances owed (referred to as liabilities).

Tips For Compiling Your Net Worth Statement

- Make sure the account names listed match the company name shown at the top of the statements they reference. For example, if you have a Roth IRA statement from E-trade, list it on the Net Worth Statement as E-trade Roth IRA, followed by your name.

- Specify account ownership type in the account names whenever possible. For example, if you have a joint investment account at Fidelity, list it as a Joint Fidelity account on the Net Worth Statement.

- If applicable, you may want to itemize the contents of your safe deposit box at the bank and file that list in your banking file. Unless there are items like jewelry, coins, etc., the safe deposit box items (often mainly documents) are often not listed on the Net Worth Statement.

Step 10
The First Month:
Meet With Your Estate Planning Attorney

Meet with your estate planning attorney during the first month to address the legal obligations of the personal representative and/or successor trustee, as well as to better understand the estate settling details and process.

1. If you do not have an estate planning attorney, find one through a referral from family, friends, co-workers or neighbors. It is helpful to work with someone recommended by a person you know.
2. Don't be tempted to ask family, a friend or a church member who happens to be a lawyer to draft documents or assist with the settlement process. If they do not specialize in estate planning as their primary practice, steer clear!
3. Every state has potentially different laws and probate can be different by county as well, so work with someone who's local, licensed and specializes in estate planning in your state.

Estate Settling Terminology To Ask Your Attorney About

- **Bequest**
  A gift of money or property given through a will.
- **Creditors**
  Individuals or businesses owed money by an estate.
- **Executor**
  Person named in a will to carry out its instructions. Female is executrix. Also called a personal representative.
- **Probate**
  The legal process of validating a will, paying debts, and distributing assets after death. Assets that go through probate usually include items you own in your name and those paid to your estate. In contrast, assets owned by a trust, or jointly with rights of survivorship, or payable-on-death or transfer-on-death, or insurance or other assets with beneficiary designations will not require probate. There are legal, executor, appraisal fees and court costs when an estate goes through probate. Probate fees are paid from assets in the estate before the assets are fully distributed to heirs.

Step 11
The First Month:
Miscellaneous "To Dos"

1. Go to the DMV (Department of Motor Vehicles) to cancel driver's license and transfer vehicle title.
2. Notify the Registrar of Voters.
3. Cancel any medication prescriptions, print subscriptions, and memberships.
4. Delete online personal accounts: email, social media, business sites, etc., to avoid fraud or identity theft. Procedures for each will vary.
5. Send out acknowledgments for cards, donations, etc., if you've decided that is something you want to do. This can also be delayed until a time that you are ready and able to tackle this project.
6. Contact the Post Office with forwarding information, if necessary.
7. Cancel all services no longer needed, i.e. phone, internet, cable, etc.

Getting Ready To Meet With Advisors

One of the most time-consuming financial aspects after someone has passed away is gathering all the documents that need to be assembled (unless they are organized in advance in a primary location).

- Death certificate(s)
- Will and/or trust
- Insurance policies (life, homeowners, health, disability, auto, etc.)
- Last credit card statements
- Investment account statements (IRAs, 401(k) plans, mutual funds, pensions, etc.)
- Last checking and savings account statements (including CDs and money-market accounts)
- Last mortgage statement
- Last two years' tax returns
- Marriage and birth certificates (of the deceased's spouse and children as well)
- An up-to-date credit report of the deceased

Step 12
The Next Few Months:
Sit Down With Your Tax Advisor

The IRS requires a final accounting after a death, and it's up to the executor or survivors to file the paperwork, so you need to see a tax advisor experienced in this area. Tax laws change, but in general, you need to discuss:

1. When a taxpayer dies, the taxpayer's estate may need to file a final return. Income will either be reported on the estate return, the return of the beneficiary who receives the income, or the tax payer's final return.
2. Money you inherit is generally not subject to income tax. Only interest earned from the time you become the owner is taxed.
3. A major exception to the general rule that inheritances are not subject to income tax is that money in traditional IRAs, employer-sponsored retirement plans (i.e. 401(k), 403(b), etc.) and annuities is taxed to the heir at the time of distribution, unless they are Roth IRAs.
4. There are many details involved (filing deadlines, cost basis, home sale rules, etc.) that must be considered and tax laws change. Talk to a tax expert for advice.

Working With A Tax Advisor

- Understand your filing status and deadlines. For the year in which the death occurs, the deceased's income taxes will be due on the normal filing date of the next year, unless extended. If you're the spouse of the deceased, you can still file a joint return for the year of death as long as you have not remarried.
- Ask about the differences in estate tax (federal and state), inheritance tax (only applicable in some states) and income tax, and their filing due dates.
- Discuss when disclaiming property as a beneficiary may be appropriate to consider.
- Bring your expense log and receipts with you to the meeting to help verify all deductions available.

Step 13
The Next Few Months:
Finalize Updated Documents With Your
Estate Planning Attorney

If you are a surviving spouse, update your estate planning documents with any new personal requests and get recommendations on new beneficiary designations.

1. You will likely need to continue meeting with the attorney for the ongoing estate settlement process, but also schedule a meeting to address updating your will/trust and power of attorney documents.
2. Your attorney will give you lots of options to think about (charitable, children/their spouses and grandchildren, gifting, etc.), so plan to take some time to digest that information and set another appointment to re-discuss before the attorney finalizes the updated documents.
3. You can always update your estate planning documents for a smaller fee (codicil of a will or amendment of a trust) later, so be aware that nothing you decide now is written in stone and can be changed again later.

Estate Planning Document Reminders

- Going forward, you should review estate planning documents every 3-5 years, whenever there has been a law change, or whenever you have had a change in your circumstances.
- The best resource for this legal advice is an attorney who specializes in estate planning and is licensed in your state of residence.
- Attorneys will remind you that you can write, date and sign a separate list (Disposition of Personal Property) at any time to attach to your estate planning documents. This list itemizes things you specifically want to go to certain people (i.e. china to daughter, gun to son, piano to school, etc.)

Step 14
The Next Few Months:
Re-evaluate Your Situation With A
Financial Advisor

The advisor who can help you after your
meetings with the tax and legal advisors, plow
through much of the paperwork with you, and
make more sense of the big picture is a Certified
Financial Planner, so make an appointment with
one.

1. Reviewing income and expense needs are
    often your most immediate priorities. A
    financial plan is a comprehensive tool
    that can help address the short-term, as
    well as long-term income needs.
2. Immediate decisions regarding retirement
    account rollovers, annuity continuation or
    payout options, Social Security claims,
    life insurance proceeds, and required
    minimum distribution planning (if over
    age 70 ½) can all be analyzed for advice
    based on your situation.
3. Investment and insurance needs should
    be discussed.
4. Assistance with re-titling accounts and
    updating beneficiary designations will
    need to be completed together.

Working With A Financial Advisor

- Statistically, a majority of women leave the financial advisor they were working with when their spouse was alive within two years after death because they didn't feel connected or comfortable with that advisor.
- Check with those you know for recommendations (the tax and legal advisors can be a good referral source too) to someone who is not only knowledgeable and experienced, but also caring and trustworthy.
- Just like hiring anyone for their professional services, be sure you meet with two or three to understand their experience, investment philosophy, fee structure and approach to working with clients.

Step 15
Ongoing:
Take Care Of Yourself

No matter what your relationship was with the person you lost, those memories, along with the financial role you are now involved in, will require some healing. Remember to take care of yourself through this process.

1. Everyone is affected differently by stress and we all choose to de-stress in various ways as well. Make time for your preferred method (yoga, meditation, walking, prayer, etc.).
2. Reading articles or books about grief can help you understand some of your feelings better, as well as realize that what you are going through is normal.
3. Talk with family or those close to you about your thoughts and let them know if there are ways they can help. Allow yourself to grieve.
4. Joining a support group or working with a counselor (or both) could be something you might at least try for a period of time for your own healing.

Ideas That Have Helped Others Who Are Grieving

Something as basic as staying hydrated, eating well and getting enough sleep is very important. It's good for your general health and can help you think clearly through all the actions and decision-making you are involved in.

- Cry as often as you need to, it's an emotional release.
- Write, in whatever format helps you, a journal, poems, letters you may or may not send.
- Ask for help, perhaps with errands, grocery shopping, pet chores, meals.
- Breathe deeply, meditate, pray, or just sit quietly and take deep breaths.
- End each day with thoughts about what you are thankful for, keep a gratitude journal, notice the little things daily.

You've finished. Before you go…

Tweet/share that you finished this book.

Please star rate this book.

Reviews are solid gold to writers. Please take a few minutes to give us some itty bitty feedback on this book.

ABOUT THE AUTHOR

Marie Burns started her career helping people balance their diet and exercise as a Registered Dietitian. A dozen years later, she began her journey as a Certified Financial Planner™ Professional and has been helping people balance their finances for almost two decades. Both roles involve guiding others to make behavior changes.

As the oldest of four children as well as the mother of four children, she is a natural fit for serving others as their "financial mother." Coming into the financial industry as a second career has helped Marie avoid the lingo of finance-speak and instead focus on translating complex subjects into understandable English.

When Marie realized that she was getting questions DAILY from friends, clients, and family related to helping aging parents, settling family estates, and couples worrying about how things will go when one of them is no longer around, she knew she needed to write a financial checklist.

Marie's goal is to create The Ripple Effect: these financial checklist books act like a rock launched into a pond and its ripples reach many more lives than she could ever positively impact in person. Marie writes and speaks to groups at www.MindMoneyMotion.com. She advises clients at www.FocusPointPlanning.com.

If you liked this Itty Bitty® Book, you might also enjoy…

Your Amazing Itty Bitty® Staying Young At Any Age Book – Dianna Whitley

Your Amazing Itty Bitty® Eldercare Book – John Smith, RN

Your Amazing Itty Bitty® Sexuality for Seniors Book – Randy and Dr. Jenny Dickason

And many other Itty Bitty® Books
available online.